PRAYERS
AND
BLESSINGS
for
DAILY LIFE
in CHRIST

PRAYERS AND BLESSINGS for DAILY LIFE in CHRIST

Compiled from Catholic Tradition
past and present.

Fr. Michael Scanlan, T.O.R.
Fr. John P. Bertolucci

Franciscan University Press
Franciscan University of Steubenville
Steubenville, OH 43952

Nihil Obstat
Daniel Sinisi, T.O.R., M.A., S.T.L.

Imprimatur
Very Rev. Edmund Carroll, T.O.R.
Minister Provincial

Cover Design: Art Mancuso
Copyright © 1983
Copyright © 1989 Revised Edition, Franciscan University
Press, All rights reserved.
Published by:
  Franciscan University Press
  Franciscan University of Steubenville
  Steubenville, OH 43952
ISBN 0-940535-00-9

TABLE OF CONTENTS

SAN DAMIANO CROSS

The San Damiano Cross is a reproduction of the one that St. Francis prayed before when he received the commission from the Lord to rebuild the Church. Franciscans cherish this cross as the symbol of their mission from God. The original cross presently hangs in Santa Chiarra (St. Clare) Church in Assisi, Italy.

At Franciscan University of Steubenville, we hold the San Damiano Cross in very special reverence. It represents to us both our tradition as Franciscan and our mission today to be committed with our lives and resources to renew and rebuild the Church in the power of God.

We have placed these crosses in central places in our chapels and around our campus. We are inspired to greater faith and commitment through our reflections and prayers before these crosses.

INTRODUCTION

We believe that the Holy Spirit anoints particular prayers and blessings in a special way. We believe that many of the prayers and blessings in this booklet were inspired by the Holy Spirit and have borne fruit through the ages. Other prayers and blessings have been inspired by the Spirit in the renewal of the church in our age and should be available to all the faithful. Finally, we believe it is very important that both priests and laity regularly use blessings in the power of the Holy Spirit for the persons, places and things which they encounter daily.

The standard for selecting these prayers and blessings was the regularity of their use by us within our ministries. In some cases we composed the prayers under the inspiration of the Holy Spirit. The origin of traditional prayers and blessings is given whenever it could be determined.

Special thanks are given to Father Philip T. Weller for permission to use blessings from the *Roman Ritual.*

In this revised and expanded version, we have included novenas and other traditional prayers which many find helpful for particular situations or circumstances.

* *Prayers originating with Fr. John Bertolucci*
+ *Prayers originating with Fr. Michael Scanlan*

O LORD, I CALL TO YOU;
  COME QUICKLY TO ME.
HEAR MY VOICE
  WHEN I CALL TO YOU.
MAY MY PRAYER BE SET
  BEFORE YOU LIKE INCENSE;
MAY THE LIFTING UP OF MY HANDS
  BE LIKE THE EVENING SACRIFICE.

Psalm 141:1-2

PRAYERS FOR EVERYDAY

PRAYER TO THE HOLY SPIRIT

Come Holy Spirit, fill the hearts of your faithful and kindle in them the fire of your love.

V. Send forth your Spirit, and they shall be created.

R. And you shalt renew the face of the earth.

Let us pray

O God, who instructs the hearts of the faithful by the light of the Holy Spirit, grant that, by the gift of the same Spirit, we may be always truly wise, and ever rejoice in His consolation, through Christ Our Lord. Amen.

Partial indulgence*

THE LORD'S PRAYER

Our Father, Who art in heaven, hallowed be Thy name; Thy kingdom come; Thy will be done on earth as it is in heaven. Give us this day our daily bread; and forgive us our trespasses as we forgive those who trespass against us; and lead us not into temptation, but deliver us from evil. Amen.

GLORY BE TO THE FATHER

Glory be to the Father, and to the Son, and to the Holy Spirit. As it was in the beginning, is now, and ever shall be, world without end. Amen.

*For an explanation of Indulgences, see page 80.

APOSTLES CREED

I believe in God, the Father Almighty, Creator of heaven and earth. And in Jesus Christ, His only Son, our Lord: who was conceived by the Holy Spirit, born of the Virgin Mary, suffered under Pontius Pilate, was crucified, died, and was buried; He descended into hell; the third day He rose again from the dead; He ascended into heaven; sits at the right hand of God the Father Almighty; from thence He shall come to judge the living and the dead. I believe in the Holy Spirit, the holy Catholic Church, the communion of Saints, the forgiveness of sins, the resurrection of the body, and life everlasting. Amen.

Partial indulgence

PRAYER BEFORE MEALS

Bless us, O Lord, and these your gifts which we are about to receive from your bounty through Christ our Lord. Amen.

Partial indulgence

PRAYER AFTER MEALS

We give you thanks, Almighty God, for all your blessings: who lives and reigns forever and ever. Amen.

Partial indulgence

MORNING⁺

O Lord, bless this day at its beginning that it may be a day given to your honor and glory. Grant to us, O Lord, the wisdom and strength to live righteously and fruitfully during all of the hours before us, through Christ our Lord. Amen.

MIDDAY⁺

Sustain us, O Lord, as we pause in the middle of this day. We turn to you as Our God, Our Protector, Our Lord and the beginning and end of our lives. We praise you and commit to you our efforts of the morning past and the day to come, through Christ Our Lord. Amen.

EVENING⁺

O Lord, Our God, in this time of evening, we give to you all that has transpired during the day. May your grace complete what has taken place so that it may best serve your kingdom. Grant to us your protection in this evening time that it may bring rest and refreshment. Protect us by your holy angels and be our guardian so that the temptations and wiles of Satan do not disrupt our lives or impede our work. We pray in the name of Jesus Our Lord. Amen.

ACT OF FAITH

O my God, I firmly believe that you are one God in three divine persons, Father, Son and Holy Spirit; I believe that your Divine Son became man and died for our sins and that He will come to judge the living and the dead. I believe these and all the truths which the holy, Catholic Church teaches because you revealed them who can neither deceive nor be deceived.

Partial indulgence

ACT OF HOPE

O my God, relying on your infinite goodness and promises, I hope to obtain pardon of my sins, the help of your grace and life everlasting through the merits of Jesus Christ, my Lord and Redeemer.

Partial indulgence

ACT OF LOVE

O my God, I love you above all things with my whole heart and soul because you are all good and worthy of all love. I love my neighbor as myself for the love of you. I forgive all who have injured me and I ask pardon of all whom I have injured.

Partial indulgence

ACT OF CONTRITION

O my God, I repent with my whole heart of all my sins, and I detest them, because I have deserved the loss of heaven and the pains of hell, but most of all, because I have offended you, infinite goodness. I firmly resolve with the help of your grace, which I pray you to grant me now and always, to confess my sins, to do penance and rather to die than offend you again. Amen.

Partial indulgence

PRAYER BEFORE AN EVENT

Direct, we beg you, O Lord, our actions by your holy inspirations, and carry them on by your gracious assistance, that every prayer and work of ours may begin always with you, and through you be happily ended. Amen.

Partial Indulgence

SHORT PRAYER OF COMMITMENT*

Jesus, I repent of my sins.
I renounce the evil one and all his works.
I surrender my life to you and I truly
    accept you as the Son of the Living God.
I receive you now into my life as my
    personal Lord and Savior.
Fill me with your Holy Spirit. I love you,
    Jesus.

PRAYER OF COMMITMENT*

Jesus, I love you.

I am sorry for my sins.

I thank you for dying on the cross for me
personally.

I celebrate your Resurrection this
beautiful day by giving my life to
you.

I invite you into my life, into my
home, into my business, into my
school, into my recreation, into
wherever I am.

Come, Lord Jesus.

I truly accept you as my Lord and God
and my personal Savior.

Come now and fill me with your
Spirit;

Fill me Lord Jesus with your Holy
Spirit.

Fill me Lord Jesus with your love and
send me forth to my family and friends,
to be able to share with them your love
and your concern.

Jesus, I love you and I shall follow you
as your disciple every day of my life.

Amen.

TO BE A DISCIPLE OF
JESUS CHRIST[+]

*"He will baptize you with the Holy Spirit
and with fire."* Matt 3:11

Lord God, you who provide the fire for a transformed life, I come before you this day and beg for the fire of your love and mercy to forgive my sins and free me from my self-imposed bondages.

I pray for the fire of your Spirit to lead me in repentance and conversion so I may be faithful in following you.

I pray for the fire of your love to ignite my heart with love for my brothers and sisters and lead me to intercede in faith for them.

I pray for the fire of faith to be committed to you and your teaching as a servant to His Master.

I pray for the fire of your desire to save all mankind to inflame me so that I can witness to the Good News of Jesus Christ and be a channel for the salvation of mankind.

Lord, I want to burn for you before all peoples. Amen.

Jesus, meek and humble of heart, make my heart like unto Thine.

PRAYER OF PETITION*

Lord Jesus Christ, Risen Savior, King of Kings, Son of God, Son of man, I come before you just as I am, acknowledging my sinfulness and my personal weaknesses. Without you I am nothing, with you, I have everything.

O Master, I ask for an increase in faith, hope and love. With praise and thanksgiving I place before you the following needs.

(Here ask for whatever you need, little or big, spiritual or material. Don't hesitate to ask Jesus for anything, He loves you.)

O Risen Lord, I offer you my life and I truly accept you as my Lord and my God. I surrender to you as my personal Savior and I repent of my sins. I am sorry for having offended you. I unite my sufferings with yours on the cross and I ask to be more deeply unified with you in your Resurrection.

Give me good health in body, soul and spirit. Let your Holy Spirit dwell within my heart. Allow me to experience your Father's love. As you lived with Mary and Joseph, so live within my home and bless every member of my family. I declare you the Lord of my house and ask for the protection of your Precious Blood over my loved ones.

I love you, Jesus Christ; I praise you Lord. I shall follow you as your disciple every day of my life. Through your Spirit, your Bible and your Church, teach me your ways. I desire to live in you, with you, for you and through you, my Risen Lord, now and forever. Amen.

CHAPLET OF DIVINE MERCY

Say this prayer on ordinary rosary beads.
"First say one 'Our Father,' 'Hail Mary' *and* 'I believe.'
Then on the large beads say the following:
Eternal Father, I offer you the Body and Blood, Soul and Divinity of your dearly beloved Son, Our Lord Jesus Christ, in atonement for our sins and those of the whole world.
On the smaller beads say:
For the sake of His sorrowful Passion have mercy on us and on the whole world.
In conclusion say three times:
'Holy God, Holy Mighty One, Holy Immortal One, have mercy on us and on the whole world.' "

THE JESUS PRAYER

Lord Jesus Christ, Son of the living God, have mercy on me a sinner.

THE UNIVERSAL PRAYER

ATTRIBUTED TO POPE CLEMENT XI

Lord, I believe in you: increase my faith.

I trust in you: strengthen my trust.

I love you: let me love you more and
more.

I am sorry for my sins: deepen my
sorrow.

I worship you as my first beginning,

I long for you as my last end,

I praise you as my constant helper, and
call on you as my loving protector.

Guide me by your wisdom,
Correct me with your justice,
Comfort me with your mercy,
Protect me with your power.

I offer you, Lord, my thoughts: to be
fixed on you;

My words: to have you for their theme;

My actions: to reflect my love for you;

My sufferings: to be endured for your
greater glory.

I want to do what you ask of me:
In the way you ask,
For as long as you ask,
Because you ask it.

Lord, enlighten my understanding
Strengthen my will,

Purify my heart, and make me holy.

Help me to repent of my past sins and
to resist temptation in the future.

Help me to rise above my human
   weaknesses and to grow stronger as a
   Christian.
Let me love you, my Lord and my
   God, and see myself as I really am:
      a pilgrim in this world,
      a Christian called to respect
      and love
   all whose lives I touch,
      those in authority over me
      or those under my authority,
      my friends and my enemies.
Help me to conquer anger with gentleness,
   Greed by generosity,
   Apathy by fervor.
Help me to forget myself and reach out
   toward others.
Make me prudent in planning,
   courageous in taking risks.
Make me patient in suffering,
   unassuming in prosperity.
Keep me, Lord, attentive at prayer,
   Temperate in food and drink,
   Diligent in my work,
   Firm in my good intentions.
Let my conscience be clear,
   my conduct without fault,
   my speech blameless,
   my life well-ordered.
Put me on guard against my human
   weaknesses.

Let me cherish your love for me,
Keep your law, and
Come at last to your Salvation.
Teach me to realize that this world is
passing,
That my true future is the happiness of
heaven,
That life on earth is short,
And the life to come eternal.
Help me to prepare for death with a
proper fear of judgment, but a
greater trust in your goodness.
Lead me safely through death to the
endless joy of heaven.
Grant this through Christ our Lord.
Amen.

PRAYER OF
ST. FRANCIS OF ASSISI

LORD,

Make me an instrument of your PEACE.

Where there is hatred, let me sow
LOVE.

Where there is injury, PARDON.

Where there is doubt, FAITH.

Where there is despair, HOPE.

Where there is darkness, LIGHT.

And where there is sadness, JOY.

O DIVINE MASTER,

Grant that I may not so much seek

To be consoled, as to CONSOLE.

To be understood, as to UNDERSTAND.

To be loved as to LOVE.

FOR it is in GIVING that we receive,

It is in PARDONING

That we are pardoned

And it is in dying

That we are born to ETERNAL LIFE.

TO THE HOLY SPIRIT

On my knees before the great cloud of witnesses, I offer myself soul and body to You, Eternal Spirit of God. I adore the brightness of Your purity, the unerring keenness of Your justice, and the might of Your love. You are the strength and the light of my soul; in You I live and move and am; I desire never to grieve You by unfaithfulness to grace, and I pray with all my heart to be kept from the smallest sin against You. Make me faithful in every thought and grant that I may always listen to Your voice, watch for Your light, and follow Your gracious inspirations. I cling to You and give myself to You and ask You by Your compassion to watch over me in my weakness. Holding the pierced feet of Jesus, and looking at His five wounds and trusting to His precious blood, and adoring His opened side and stricken heart, I implore You, Adorable Spirit, helper of my infirmity, so to keep me in Your grace that I may never sin against You with the sin which You cannot forgive.

Give me grace, O Holy Spirit, Spirit of the Father and the Son, to say to You always and everywhere, "Speak, Lord, for Your servant heareth."

O Spirit of Wisdom, preside over all my thoughts, words, and actions, from this hour till the moment of my death.

Spirit of Understanding, enlighten and teach me.

Spirit of Counsel, direct my inexperience.

Spirit of Fortitude, strengthen my weakness.

Spirit of Knowledge, instruct my ignorance.

Spirit of Piety, make me fervent in good works.

Spirit of Fear, restrain me from all evil.

Spirit of Peace, give me Your peace.

Heavenly Spirit, make me persevere in the service of God, and enable me to act on all occasions with goodness and benignity, patience, charity, and joy, longanimity, mildness and fidelity. Let the heavenly virtues of modesty, continency, and chastity adorn the temple You have chosen for Your abode. O Spirit of Holiness, by Your all-powerful grace, preserve my soul from the misfortune of sin. Amen.

TE DEUM

You are God: we praise you;
You are the Lord: we acclaim you;
You are the eternal Father:
All creation worships you.
To you all angels, all the powers of heaven,
Cherubim and Seraphim, sing in endless
    praise:
  Holy, holy, holy, Lord, God of power
  and might,
  heaven and earth are full of your glory.
The glorious company of apostles praise
    you.
The noble fellowship of prophets praise you.
The white-robed army of martyrs praise
    you.
Throughout the world the holy Church
    acclaims you:
  Father, of majesty unbounded,
  your true and only Son, worthy of all
  worship,
  and the Holy Spirit, advocate and guide.
You, Christ, are the king of glory,
the eternal Son of the Father.
When you became man to set us free
you did not spurn the Virgin's womb.
You overcame the sting of death,
and opened the kingdom of heaven to all
believers.

You are seated at God's right hand in glory.
We believe that you will come, and be our judge.
Come then, Lord, and help your people, bought with the price of your own blood, and bring us with your saints to glory everlasting.
V. Save your people, Lord, and bless your inheritance.
R. Govern and uphold them now and always.
V. Day by day we bless you.
R. We praise your name for ever.
V. Keep us today, Lord, from all sin.
R. Have mercy on us, Lord, have mercy.
V. Lord, show us your love and mercy;
R. for we put our trust in you.
V. In you, Lord, is our hope:
R. and we shall never hope in vain.

Partial indulgence when said in thanksgiving.
Plenary indulgence when recited publicly on last day of the year.

THE DIVINE PRAISES

Blessed be God.

Blessed be His holy Name.

Blessed be Jesus Christ, true God and
  true Man.

Blessed be the Name of Jesus.

Blessed be His most Sacred Heart.

Blessed be His most precious Blood.

Blessed be Jesus in the most holy Sacrament
  of the altar.

Blessed be the Holy Spirit, the Paraclete.

Blessed be the great Mother of God, Mary most
  holy.

Blessed be her holy and Immaculate Conception.

Blessed be her glorious Assumption.

Blessed be the name of Mary, Virgin and
  Mother.

Blessed be St. Joseph, her most chaste spouse.

Blessed be God in His angels and in His saints.

LITANY OF THE SACRED HEART

Lord, have mercy on us.

Christ, have mercy on us.

Lord, have mercy on us.

Christ, hear us.

Christ, graciously hear us.

God the Father of Heaven, have mercy on us.

God the Son, Redeemer of the world, have mercy on us.

God the Holy Spirit, have mercy on us.

Holy Trinity, one God, have mercy on us.

Heart of Jesus, Son of the Eternal Father,

Heart of Jesus, formed by the Holy Ghost in the womb of the Virgin Mother,

Heart of Jesus, substantially united to the Word of God,

Heart of Jesus, of infinite majesty,

Heart of Jesus, sacred temple of God,

Heart of Jesus, tabernacle of the Most High,

Heart of Jesus, house of God and gate of Heaven,

Heart of Jesus, glowing furnace of charity,

Heart of Jesus, abode of justice and love,

Heart of Jesus, full of goodness and love,

Heart of Jesus, abyss of all virtues,

Heart of Jesus, most worthy of all praise,

Have mercy on us.

Heart of Jesus, King and center of all
hearts,

Heart of Jesus, in whom are all the
treasures of wisdom and knowledge,

Heart of Jesus, in whom dwells the fullness of divinity.

Heart of Jesus, in whom the Father is
well pleased,

Heart of Jesus, of whose fullness we
have all received,

Heart of Jesus, desire of the everlasting
hills,

Heart of Jesus, patient and most merciful.

Heart of Jesus, enriching all who invoke
Thee,

Heart of Jesus, fountain of life and
holiness,

Heart of Jesus, propitiation for our sins,

Heart of Jesus, loaded down with op-
probrium,

Heart of Jesus, bruised for our offenses,

Heart of Jesus, obedient unto death,

Heart of Jesus, pierced with a lance,

Heart of Jesus, source of all consolation,

Heart of Jesus, our life and resurrection,

Heart of Jesus, our peace and reconcil-
iation,

Heart of Jesus, victim for sins,

Have mercy on us.

28

Heart of Jesus, salvation of those who
  trust in you,
Heart of Jesus, hope of those who die
  in you,
Heart of Jesus, delight of all the saints,

Lamb of God, who takes away the sins of the world, *spare us, O Lord.*

Lamb of God, who takes away the sins of the world, *graciously hear us, O Lord.*

Lamb of God, who takes away the sins of the world, *have mercy on us.*

V. Jesus, meek and humble of heart.

R. Make our hearts like unto yours.

Let us pray

Almighty and everlasting God, look upon the Heart of your well-beloved Son and upon the praise and satisfaction which He offers unto you in the name of sinners, and in your great goodness grant them pardon when they seek your mercy, in the name of your Son, Jesus Christ, who lives and reigns with you forever and ever. Amen.

PRAYER BEFORE A CRUCIFIX

Look down upon me, good and gentle Jesus, while before your face I humbly kneel, and with burning soul pray and beseech you to fix deep in my heart lively sentiments of faith, hope and charity, true contrition for my sins, and a firm purpose of amendment while I contemplate with deep love and tender pity your five wounds, pondering over them within me, calling to mind the words which David, your prophet, said of you, my good Jesus: *"They have pierced my hands and my feet; they have numbered all my bones."*

Ps. 22:17-18   *Partial indulgence*

Plenary indulgence after Communion before an image of Christ Crucified on each Friday of Lent and Passover.

O Sacrament, most holy, O Sacrament divine. All praise and all thanksgiving be every moment Thine.

A SPIRITUAL COMMUNION

"A spiritual communion acts on the soul as blowing does on a fire which is about to go out. Whenever you feel your love of God growing cold, quickly make a spiritual communion," said the Cure of Ars.

O Jesus, I turn toward the holy tabernacle where You live hidden for love of me. I love you, O my God. I cannot receive you in Holy Communion. Come nevertheless and visit me with Your grace. Come spiritually into my heart. Purify it. Sanctify it. Render it like unto Your own. Amen.

OR

O my Jesus, I believe that you are present in the most holy Sacrament. I love you above all things and desire to receive you into my soul; but since I cannot receive you sacramentally, come spiritually into my heart. Heal my sinful soul. Feed me for I am hungry. Strengthen me for I am weak. Enliven and sanctify me with your precious body and blood now, and especially at the hour of my death.   *Partial indulgence*

PRAYER BEFORE COMMUNION

ST. THOMAS AQUINAS

Almighty and ever-living God,
I approach the sacrament of your only-
begotten Son, our Lord Jesus Christ.
I come sick to the doctor of life,
unclean to the fountain of mercy,
blind to the radiance of eternal light,
and poor and needy to the Lord of
heaven and earth.
Lord, in your great generosity, heal
my sickness, wash away my defilement,
enlighten my blindness, enrich my
poverty, and clothe my nakedness.
May I receive the bread of angels, the
King of kings and Lord of lords, with
humble reverence, with the purity and
faith, the repentance and love, and the
determined purpose that will help to
bring me to salvation.
May I receive the sacrament of the
Lord's body and blood, and its
reality and power.
Kind God, may I receive the body of
your only-begotten Son, our Lord
Jesus Christ, born from the womb of
the Virgin Mary, and so be received
into his mystical body and numbered
among his members.

Loving Father, as on my earthly pilgrimage I now receive your beloved Son under the veil of a sacrament, may I one day see him face to face in glory, who lives and reigns with you forever. Amen.

THANKSGIVING AFTER COMMUNION

Lord, God, Father and Creator of all that is, I thank you for the blessings in my life. I know that it has pleased you to give us a Kingdom, to send Jesus to manifest your love, to die and rise for us to reign in our hearts through the power of the Holy Spirit. I thank you for the good news of the gospel, for forgiveness, for knowledge of salvation, for the first pledge of our inheritance as adopted sons and daughters, for the glory you give to us and the fullness of eternal glory promised to us. Lord, bless us with grateful hearts to see you in all beauty, all goodness, and all of creation so that we might participate each day in the hymn of praise destined for all your beloved forever and ever without end. Amen.

THANKSGIVING AFTER MASS

ST. THOMAS AQUINAS

Lord, Father, all-powerful and ever-living
  God,
I thank you, for even though I am a
  sinner, your unprofitable servant,
  not because of my worth, but in the
  kindness of your mercy, you have fed
  me with the precious body and blood
  of your Son, our Lord Jesus Christ.
I pray that this Holy Communion may
  not bring me condemnation and
  punishment but forgiveness and
  salvation.
May it be a helmet of faith and a
  shield of good will.
May it purify me from evil ways and
  put an end to my evil passions.
May it bring me charity and patience,
  humility and obedience, and growth in
  the power to do good.
May it be my strong defense against all
  my enemies, visible and invisible, and
  the perfect calming of all my evil
  impulses, bodily and spiritual.
May it unite me more closely to you,
  the one true God, and lead me safely
  through death to everlasting happiness
  with you.

And I pray that you will lead me, a
   sinner, to the banquet where you,
   with your Son and Holy Spirit, are
   true and perfect light, total fulfillment,
   everlasting joy, gladness without end,
   and perfect happiness to your saints.
Grant this through Christ our Lord.
   Amen.

PRAYER TO OUR REDEEMER

Soul of Christ, make me holy.
Body of Christ, be my salvation.
Blood of Christ, let me drink your wine.
Water flowing from the side of
   Christ, wash me clean.
Passion of Christ, strengthen me.
Kind Jesus, hear my prayer;
Hide me within your wounds and keep
   me close to you.
Defend me from the evil enemy.
Call me at my death to the fellowship
   of your saints, that I may sing your
   praise with them through all eternity.
   Amen.   *Partial indulgence*

My Lord and my God.

PRAYERS OF DELIVERANCE

PRAYER TO ST. MICHAEL

St. Michael, the archangel, defend us in the day of battle. Be our protection against the wickedness and snares of the devil. May God rebuke him, we humbly pray, and do thou, O Prince of the heavenly hosts by the power of God, drive into hell Satan and all the other evil spirits who prowl through the world seeking the ruin of souls. Amen.

PROTECTION FROM DANGER⁺

O Lord, you are our protector and defender. We turn to you and praise your name in this moment of danger. Bless us O Lord with your grace, surround us with your holy angels and guide us in your Holy Spirit that we may emerge from this danger in the fullness of health and well being so as to praise and serve you all the days of our lives. Amen.

LITANY OF THE
MOST PRECIOUS BLOOD OF JESUS

Lord, have mercy,
    Christ have mercy.
Lord, have mercy.
Christ hear us.
    Christ graciously hear us.

God, the Father of heaven, have mercy
on us.
God the Son, Redeemer of the world,
have mercy on us.
God the Holy Spirit, have mercy on us.
Holy Trinity, one God, have mercy on us.
Blood of Christ, only-begotten Son of the
eternal Father; Save us.
Blood of Christ, incarnate Word of God,
Blood of Christ, of the new and eternal
Testament,
Blood of Christ, falling upon the earth in
the agony,
Blood of Christ, shed profusely in the
scourging,
Blood of Christ, flowing forth in the
crowning with thorns,
Blood of Christ, poured out on the cross,
Blood of Christ, price of our salvation,
Blood of Christ, without which there is no
forgiveness,
Blood of Christ, Eucharistic drink and
refreshment of souls,
Blood of Christ, stream of mercy,
Blood of Christ, victor over demons,
Blood of Christ, courage of martyrs,
Blood of Christ, strength of confessors,
Blood of Christ, bringing forth virgins,
Blood of Christ, help of those in peril,
Blood of Christ, relief of the burdened,
Blood of Christ, solace in sorrow,
Blood of Christ, hope of the penitent,

Save us.

Blood of Christ, consolation of the
   dying

Blood of Christ, peace and tenderness of
   hearts,

Blood of Christ, pledge of eternal life,

Blood of Christ, freeing souls from
   purgatory,

Blood of Christ, most worthy of all glory
   and honor.

Save us.

Lamb of God, you take away the sins
   of the world; spare us, O Lord.

Lamb of God, you take away the sins
   of the world; graciously hear us, O
   Lord.

Lamb of God, you take away the sins
   of the world; have mercy on us.

V. You have redeemed us, O Lord, in
   your Blood.

R. And made us, for our God, a
   kingdom.

Let us pray.

Almighty and eternal God, you have
appointed your only-begotten Son the Redeemer
of the world, and willed to be appeased by his
Blood. Grant, we beg you, that we may worthily
adore this price of our salvation, and through its
power be safeguarded from the evils of the present life, so that we may rejoice in its fruits forever in heaven. Through the same Christ our
Lord, Amen.   *Partial indulgence*

PRAYER OF HEALING

Lord Jesus Christ, you are the messiah, the redeemer, the saviour, the healer and the deliverer of all mankind. I come to you today, Lord, in communion with all the angels and saints and especially with your holy mother Mary as a member of the Body of Christ. I ask you to manifest the signs and wonders of your kingdom in extension of your merciful act of redemption by healing this servant of yours who seeks to be restored to fullness of life. O Lord, bless your servant so that he/she may be a blessing to your people. Amen.

PRAYER FOR THE CRITICALLY ILL⁺

O Lord our God, you are the healer of all mankind. In your merciful love you heal us of sin and the effects of sin in this life and the next. We pray to you, our Lord, this day to accelerate your plan of healing for our loved one. Give your beloved the fullness of life here on earth or call your beloved home to glory with you for all eternity. Amen.

A PRAYER IN SUFFERING

Grant me, O Lord, the grace to unite my sufferings with yours so that I may suffer as your true follower. I do not ask to be freed from afflictions since these are the reward of the saints; but I beg of you to make me find in calmness and resignation the true use of trials.

Give me faith and hope. Take from me all that can displease you. Restore my health if such is for your glory and grant that I may adore your holy will in all that comes to me. My God, I desire, I accept, I abandon myself lovingly to your holy will.

Grant me, O Lord, the precious gift of final perseverance, that whenever my last hour shall come, I may die in your grace and friendship. All my confidence is in you; through the infinite merits of the death and passion of Jesus Christ, I humbly hope for mercy, grace, and salvation. Amen.

Sacred **Heart of Jesus, I place** my trust in Thee.

FOR THE BLESSINGS OF ETERNITY

Lord Jesus, offer to your eternal Father all the drops of that precious blood which flowed from your body in the bitter agony in the garden. Offer them in remission of my sins and for the discharge of the punishment due to them.

O Lord Jesus, offer to the eternal Father, all the anguish and pain you endured on the cross that I may obtain a happy death and release from the punishment due to my sins.

O Lord Jesus, receive me into your arms outstretched on the cross; hide me in your wounds and receive my soul into the bosom of your mercy.

O Lord Jesus, by your victory over death, show mercy to my soul and receive it into your kingdom, there to sing your praise for all eternity. Amen.

ACT OF RESIGNATION

My Lord and my God, even now I most willingly and cheerfully accept whatever form of death it will please you to send me, with all its anguish, sorrow, and pain.

Plenary indulgence at the hour of death under the usual conditions

FOR THE DECEASED

Eternal rest grant to them, O Lord, and let perpetual light shine upon them. May they rest in peace. Amen.

Partial indulgence, applicable only to the souls in purgatory.

To you, O Lord, we recommend the soul of your servant, that being dead to this world, (he, she) may live to you; and whatever sins (he, she) has committed through human frailty, we beseech you, in your goodness, mercifully to pardon. Through Christ our Lord. Amen.

O God, the Creator and Redeemer of all the faithful, grant to the souls of the servants departed the remission of all their sins, that through pious supplications they may obtain the pardon which they have always desired. Who lives and reigns world without end. Amen.

A SHORT WAY OF THE CROSS

First Station
Jesus Is Condemned to Death

O Jesus! so meek and uncomplaining, teach me resignation in trials.

Second Station
Jesus Carries His Cross

My Jesus, this Cross should be mine, not yours; my sins crucified you.

Third Station
Our Lord Falls the First Time

O Jesus! by this first fall, never let me fall into mortal sin.

Fourth Station
Jesus Meets His Mother

O Jesus! may no human tie, however dear, keep me from following the road of the Cross.

Fifth Station
*Simon the Cyrenean Helps Jesus
Carry His Cross*

Simon unwillingly assisted you; may I with patience suffer all for you.

Sixth Station
Veronica Wipes the Face of Jesus

O Jesus! You imprinted your sacred features upon Veronica's veil; stamp them also indelibly upon my heart.

Seventh Station
The Second Fall of Jesus

By your second fall, preserve me, dear Lord, from relapse into sin.

Eighth Station
Jesus Consoles the Women of Jerusalem

My greatest consolation would be to hear you say: ''Many sins are forgiven you, because you have loved much.''

Ninth Station
Third Fall of Jesus

O Jesus! when weary upon life's long journey, be my strength and my perseverance.

Tenth Station
Jesus Is Stripped of His Garments

My soul has been robbed of its robe of innocence; clothe me, dear Jesus, with the garb of penance and contrition.

Eleventh Station
Jesus Is Nailed to the Cross

You forgave your enemies; my God, teach me to forgive injuries and FORGET them.

Twelfth Station
Jesus Dies on the Cross

You are dying, my Jesus, but your Sacred Heart still throbs with love for your sinful children.

Thirteenth Station
Jesus Is Taken Down from the Cross

Receive me into your arms, O Sorrowful Mother; and obtain for me perfect contrition for my sins.

Fourteenth Station
Jesus Is Laid in the Sepulcher

When I receive you into my heart in Holy Communion, O Jesus, make it a fit abiding place for your adorable Body. Amen.

PRAYER TO WARD OFF FLOODS

God who gives saving grace even to the wicked one who does not will the death of a sinner, we humbly appeal to you in glory, asking that you protect, with your heavenly aid, your trusting servants from all perils of flood. Let them find in you a constant safeguard, so that they may always serve you and never be separated from you through any temptation; through Christ our Lord. Amen.

PRAYER FOR VOCATIONS

O God, who wills not the death of a sinner, but rather that he be converted and live, grant we beseech you, through the intercession of the Blessed Mary, ever virgin, and Saint Joseph, her spouse, and all the Saints, an increase of laborers for your Church, fellow laborers with Christ to spend and consume themselves for souls through the same Jesus Christ, your Son who lives and reigns with you in the unity of the Holy Spirit, God forever and ever. Amen.

Our Lady of Good Health

HONORING MARY AND THE SAINTS

THE HAIL MARY

Hail Mary, full of grace, the Lord is with you; blessed are you among women, and blessed is the fruit of your womb, Jesus. Holy Mary, Mother of God, pray for us sinners now and at the hour of our death. Amen.

THE MEMORARE

Remember, O most gracious virgin Mary, that never was it known that anyone who fled to your protection, implored your help or sought your intercession was left unaided. Inspired with this confidence, I fly to you, O Virgin of virgins, my Mother. To you I come, before you I stand, sinful and sorrowful. O Mother of the Word Incarnate, do not ignore my petitions, but in your mercy hear and answer me. Amen.

Partial indulgence

CONSECRATION TO THE BLESSED MOTHER

My Queen, my Mother, I give myself entirely to you, and to show my devotion to you, I consecrate to you this day, my eyes, my ears, my mouth, my heart, my whole being without reserve. Wherefore good Mother as I am your own, keep me, guard me, as your property and possession. Amen.

THE ANGELUS

V. The angel of the Lord declared unto
Mary.

R. And she conceived of the Holy Spirit.

Hail Mary, etc.

V. Behold the handmaid of the Lord.

R. Be it done unto me according to thy
word.

Hail Mary, etc.

V. And the Word was made flesh.

R. And dwelt among us.

Hail Mary, etc.

V. Pray for us, O holy Mother of God.

R. That we may be made worthy of the
promises of Christ.

Let us pray

Pour forth, we beseech You, O Lord, Your grace
into our hearts, that we to whom the Incarnation of Christ, Your Son, was made known by
the message of an angel, may by His Passion and
Cross be brought to the glory of His Resurrection, through the same Christ our Lord. Amen.

Partial indulgence

REGINA COELI

(Said during Paschaltime instead of the Angelus)

Queen of heaven, rejoice. Alleluia.
For He Whom you did bear.
Alleluia.
Has risen as He said. Alleluia.
Pray for us to God. Alleluia.
V. Rejoice and be glad, O Virgin Mary.
Alleluia.
R. For the Lord is truly risen. Alleluia.

Let us pray

O God, Who by Resurrection of your Son, our Lord Jesus Christ, has vouchsafed to give joy to the whole world; grant, we beseech you, that, through the intercession of the Virgin Mary, His Mother, we may attain the joys of eternal life. Through the same Christ, our Lord. Amen.

Partial indulgence

WE FLY TO YOUR PATRONAGE

We fly to your patronage, O holy Mother of God; despise not our petitions in our necessities, but deliver us always from all dangers, O glorious and blessed Virgin.

Holy Mary, Mother of God, Queen of Peace, pray for us. Amen.

THE LITANY OF THE
BLESSED VIRGIN MARY

Lord, have mercy on us,

Christ, have mercy on us.

Lord, have mercy on us.

Christ, hear us.

Christ, graciously hear us.

God the Father of heaven, have mercy on us.

God the Son, Redeemer of the world, have mercy on us.

God the Holy Spirit, have mercy on us.

Holy Trinity, one God, have mercy on us.

Holy Mary,

Holy Mother of God,

Holy Virgin of virgins,

Mother of Christ,

Mother of divine grace,

Mother most pure,

Mother most chaste,

Mother inviolate,

Mother undefiled,

Mother most amiable,

Mother most admirable,

Mother of good counsel,

Mother of our Creator,

Mother of our Redeemer,

Virgin most prudent,

Virgin most venerable,

Virgin most renowned,

Virgin most powerful,

Virgin most merciful,

Pray for us.

Virgin most faithful,
Mirror of justice,
Seat of wisdom,
Cause of our joy,
Spiritual vessel,
Vessel of honor,
Singular vessel of devotion,
Mystical rose,
Tower of David,
Tower of ivory,
House of gold,
Ark of the covenant,
Gate of heaven,
Morning star,
Health of the sick,
Refuge of sinners,
Comforter of the afflicted,
Help of Christians,
Queen of Angels,
Queen of Patriarchs,
Queen of Prophets,
Queen of Apostles,
Queen of Martyrs,
Queen of Confessors,
Queen of Virgins,
Queen of all Saints,
Queen conceived without original sin,
Queen assumed into Heaven,
Queen of the most holy Rosary,
Queen of peace,

Pray for us.

Lamb of God, You take away the sins of the
 world, *spare us, O Lord.*

Lamb of God, You take away the sins of the world, *graciously hear us, O Lord.*

Lamb of God, You take away the sins of the world, *have mercy on us.*

V. Pray for us, O holy Mother of God.

R. That we may be made worthy of the promises of Christ.

Let us pray

Grant us your servants, we beseech you, O Lord God, to rejoice in continual health of mind and body; and by the glorious intercession of Blessed Mary ever Virgin, to be freed from present sorrow and enjoy eternal gladness. Through Christ our Lord. Amen.   *Partial indulgence*

TO OUR LADY FOR PROTECTION OF THE HOME

Holy Mary, Virgin Mother of God, who was conceived without sin, we choose you this day as the lady and mistress of this house. We beseech you through your Immaculate Conception to preserve us from pestilence, fire, and water; from lightning and tempests; from robbers, from schisms and heresies; from earthquakes; and from sudden and unprovided death. Bless and protect us, O holy Virgin; obtain for us the grace to avoid all sin and every other misfortune and accident.

Praised forever be the most holy Sacrament of the altar! In You, O Lord, have we put our trust; let us never be confounded. Amen.

MAGNIFICAT

My soul magnifies the Lord:

And my spirit rejoices in God my Savior.

Because He has regarded the humility of His handmaid: for behold from henceforth all generations shall call me blessed.

For He that is mighty has done great things to me: and holy is His name.

And His mercy is from generation to generation, to them that fear Him.

He has shown might in His arm; He has scattered the proud in the conceit of their heart.

He has put down the mighty from their seat, and has exalted the humble.

He has filled the hungry with good things: and the rich He has sent empty away.

He has received Israel His servant, being mindful of His mercy.

As He spoke to our fathers, to Abraham, and to His seed forever.

Glory be to the Father and to the Son and to the Holy Spirit.

As it was in the beginning, is now, and ever shall be, world without end. Amen.

O Mary, conceived without sin, pray for us who have recourse to you.

THE MYSTERIES OF THE ROSARY

THE JOYFUL MYSTERIES

1. The Annunciation by the Archangel Gabriel to the Virgin Mary
2. The Visitation of the Virgin Mary to the Parents of St. John the Baptist
3. The Birth of Our Lord at Bethlehem
4. The Presentation of Our Lord in the Temple
5. The Finding of Our Lord in the Temple

THE SORROWFUL MYSTERIES

1. The Agony of Our Lord in the Garden of Gethsemane
2. The Scourging of Our Lord at the Pillar
3. The Crowning of Our Lord with Thorns
4. The Carrying of the Cross by Our Lord to Calvary
5. The Crucifixion and Death of Our Lord

THE GLORIOUS MYSTERIES

1. The Resurrection of Our Lord from the dead
2. The Ascension of Our Lord into Heaven
3. The Descent of the Holy Spirit upon the Apostles
4. The Assumption of Our Blessed Lady into Heaven
5. The Coronation of Our Blessed Lady as Queen of Heaven

HAIL, HOLY QUEEN

Hail, holy queen, mother of mercy, our life, our sweetness, and our hope. To you we cry, poor banished children of Eve; to you we send up our sighs, mourning and weeping in this valley of tears. Turn then, O most gracious advocate, your eyes of mercy toward us, and after this, our exile, show unto us the blessed fruit of your womb, Jesus. O clement, O loving, O sweet virgin Mary.

V. Pray for us, O holy mother of God;

R. That we may be made worthy of the promises of Christ. Amen.   *Partial indulgence*

Let us pray

O God, whose only begotten Son by His life, death, and resurrection has purchased for us the rewards of eternal life, grant, we beseech you, that meditating on these mysteries of the most holy rosary of the blessed Virgin Mary, we may imitate what they contain, and obtain what they promise. Through the same Christ our Lord. Amen.

O most holy Virgin, we believe and confess your holy and Immaculate Conception, pure and without stain. O most pure Virgin, by your virginal purity, Immaculate Conception, and glorious qualities as Mother of God, obtain for us from your divine Son the virtues of humility and charity; great purity of heart, body, and soul; final perseverance in good; the gift of fervor in prayer, a pious life, and a happy death.

V. O Mary, conceived without sin.

R. Pray for us who have recourse to thee.

PRAYER TO OUR LADY
OF GOOD HEALTH

Since the sixth century, the Madonna della Salute, Our Lady of Good Health, has been associated with the physician martyrs, Saints Cosmas and Damian, in prayers of intercession for health of body and salvation of soul. The icon of Our Lady of Good Health is enthroned above the main altar in the Basilica of Sts. Cosmas and Damian in the central house of the Third Order Regular Franciscans in Rome, Italy. A replica of the icon hangs in Christ the King Chapel on the campus of Franciscan University in Steubenville, Ohio.

Most holy Virgin, venerated with the title of Our Lady of Good Health, because in every age you have come to the assistance of the sick, we ask you to intercede for us, for those dear to us, and for all who are ill. Obtain for us health of mind and body or at least strength to accept our sufferings in union with Christ our Redeemer.

Mary, Health of the Sick, pray for us!

Most holy Virgin, consoler of the afflicted, we entrust to your maternal protection our brothers and sisters who are experiencing pain and isolation, those who do not believe in Christ, and those who do not hope for a new world. O Mother of Grace, we ask you to show to every person who is sick the way to salvation and happiness.

Mary, Health of the Sick, pray for us!

Most holy Virgin, Mother of our Redeemer, keep far from us and from our world the serious evil of sin and obtain that, through the intercession of the holy physician martyrs Cosmas and Damian, we may merit to live always in perfect friendship with God.

Mary, Health of the Sick, pray for us!

O Lord our God, grant to us your sons and daughters that we may enjoy ever more completely health of body and soul and, through the intercession of Mary most holy, free us from every evil and guide us to happiness that is everlasting. Amen.

GUARDIAN ANGEL

Angel of God, my guardian dear, to whom God's love commits me here. Ever this day be at my side, to light, to guard, to rule, to guide. Amen.   *Partial indulgence*

THE SAINTS

Lord God, you alone are holy
   and no one is good without you.
Through the intercession of St. N. . . .
   help us to live in such a way
   that we may not be deprived of a share
   in your glory.
We ask this through Christ our Lord.
Amen.

PRAYER TO ST. JOSEPH

To you, O blessed Joseph, do we fly in our tribulation, and having implored the help of your most holy spouse, we confidently crave your patronage also. Through that charity which bound you to the Immaculate Virgin Mother of God, and through the paternal love with which you embraced the Child Jesus, we humbly beseech you graciously to regard the inheritance which Jesus Christ has purchased by His blood, and with your power and strength to aid us in our necessities.

O most watchful guardian of the divine family, defend the chosen children of Jesus Christ. O most loving father, ward off from us every contagion of error and corrupting influence. O our most mighty protector, be propitious to us and from heaven assist us in this our struggle with the powers of darkness; and as once you rescued the Child Jesus from deadly peril, so now protect God's holy Church from the snares of the enemy and from all adversity. Shield, too, each one of us by your constant protection, so that, supported by your example and your aid, we may be able to live piously, to die holily, and to obtain eternal happiness in heaven. Amen.

Partial indulgence

NOVENA PRAYERS

IN HONOR OF THE CHILD JESUS

(For the twenty-fifth of every month)

Eternal Father, I offer to your honor and glory and for my eternal salvation and for the salvation of the whole world, the mystery of the birth of our divine Savior.

Glory be to the Father . . .

Eternal Father, I offer to your honor and glory and for my eternal salvation the sufferings of the most holy Virgin and St. Joseph in that long weary journey from Nazareth to Bethlehem; I offer you the sorrows of their hearts when they found no place to shelter themselves when the Savior of the world was to be born.

Glory be to the Father . . .

Eternal Father, I offer to your honor and glory and for my eternal salvation the sufferings of Jesus in the stable where He was born, the cold He suffered, the swaddling-clothes which bound Him, the tears He shed, and His tender infant cries.

Glory be to the Father . . .

Eternal Father, I offer to your honor and glory and for my eternal salvation the pain which the holy Child Jesus felt in His tender body when He submitted to circumcision. I offer Thee His precious blood, which then for the first time He shed for the salvation of the whole human race.

Glory be to the Father . . .

Eternal Father, I offer to your honor and glory and for my eternal salvation the humility, mortification, patience, charity, and all the virtues of the Child Jesus. I thank you and I love you and I bless you without end for the ineffable mystery of the Incarnation of the Divine Word.

Glory be to the Father . . .

V. And the Word was made flesh.

R. And dwelt among us.

Let us pray

O God, whose only-begotten Son was made manifest to us in the substance of our flesh, grant, we beseech you, that through Him whom we acknowledge to be like unto ourselves our souls may be inwardly renewed, who lives and reigns with you forever and ever. Amen.

Begin on November 30

Pray frequently during the day during Advent.

Hail and blessed be the hour and moment when the Son of God was born of the most pure Virgin in Bethlehem at midnight, in piercing cold. In that hour vouchsafe O my God, to hear my prayers and grant my desires, through the merits of our Savior Jesus Christ and of His Virgin Mother. Amen.

FEAST OF THE NATIVITY

Begin on December 16

O most holy Virgin and blessed St. Joseph, obtain for us the grace to perform this novena with such attention, devotion, and ardent charity, as will entitle us to join the angels in rendering glory to God.

> V. Let us make three aspirations to incline the Infant Jesus to turn His favorable attention on us.

O Divine Infant of Bethlehem, whom we adore and acknowledge to be our Sovereign Lord, come and take birth in our hearts. Amen.

O Infant Jesus, grant that every moment of our lives we may pay homage to that moment in which you began the work of our salvation. Amen.

O holy Mother of our Infant Savior, obtain that we may so prepare ourselves for His coming as not to be separated from Him for all eternity. Amen.

Most Holy Infant Jesus, true God and true man, our Savior and Redeemer, with all earnestness and respect, we beseech you, by that charity, humility, and bounty, which you displayed in your infancy, graciously undertaken for the love of us, that you would vouchsafe to grant us the favor we now beg, if it be for the honor of God and our salvation.

Partial indulgence

SAINT JOSEPH

Begin on March 10

We beseech you, O Lord, that we may be assisted by the merits of St. Joseph, the spouse of your most holy Mother, that what of ourselves we are unable to obtain we may receive by His intercession. Who lives and reigns world without end. Amen.

FEAST OF THE ANNUNCIATION

Begin on March 16

O God, who was pleased that your Word should take flesh at the message of an angel in the womb of the Blessed Virgin Mary, grant that we who believe her to be truly the Mother of God may be helped by her intercession with you. Through Christ our Lord. Amen.

FOR PENTECOST

Use the prayer to the Holy Spirit on page 22.
Begin nine days before the feast of Pentecost.

THE ASSUMPTION

Begin on August 6

Almighty and everlasting God, who has assumed the Immaculate Virgin Mary, the Mother of your Son, body and soul into celestial glory, grant, we beseech you that intent on heavenly things, we may always deserve to be partakers of her glory. Through Christ our Lord. Amen.

NATIVITY OF THE BLESSED VIRGIN

Begin on August 30

We beseech you, O Lord, grant to your servants the gift of your heavenly grace, so that we for whom the childbearing of the Blessed Virgin was the beginning of salvation, may, on this the joyful festival of her nativity be blessed with an increase of peace. Through Christ our Lord. Amen.

THE IMMACULATE CONCEPTION

Begin on November 29

O God, who by the Immaculate Conception of the Virgin Mary prepared a fitting dwelling-place for your Son, grant we beseech Thee, that as through the death of your Son, foreseen by you, you preserved His mother from all sin, so you would grant us also pure in heart to come to you. Through Christ our Lord. Amen.

BLESSINGS

BLESSING OF AN INFANT

Lord Jesus Christ, Son of the living God, begotten before time was, yet willing to be an infant within time; who loved childhood innocence; who deigned to embrace tenderly and to bless the little ones when they were brought to you; be ready with your dearest blessings for this child as he (she) journeys through life, and let no evil ways corrupt his (her) understanding. May he (she) advance in wisdom and grace with the years, and be enabled ever to please you, who are God, living and reigning with the Father, in the unity of the Holy Spirit, forever and ever. Amen.

BLESSING OF A CHILD

Lord Jesus Christ. Son of the living God, who said: "Let the little children come to me and do not stop them. The kingdom of God belongs to such as these," pour out the power of your blessing † on this child, and consider the faith and devotion of the Church and of its parents. Advancing in virtue and wisdom before God and men, may he (she) reach a blessed old age and finally attain everlasting salvation. We ask this of you who live and reign forever and ever. Amen.

BLESSINGS OF YOUNG CHILDREN WHO ARE SICK

God, by whose power all things grow to maturity, and once mature retain their strength, reach out your right hand to this boy (girl) who is afflicted at this tender age. Let him (her) regain health, grow up to manhood (womanhood), and serve you in gratitude and fidelity all the days of his (her) life; through Christ our Lord. Amen.

Merciful God and Father, our unalloyed comfort, who, having the interests of your creatures at heart, are inclined in your goodness to bestow the grace of healing, not only on the soul but on the body as well; be pleased to raise up this sick child from his (her) bed of suffering, and to return him (her) in full health to your Church and to his (her) parents. May he (she) then throughout the days of his (her) life, as he (she) advances in favor and knowledge in your sight and that of men, serve you in righteousness and holiness, and render you due thanks for your goodness; through Christ our Lord. Amen.

BLESSING OF AN EXPECTANT MOTHER

Lord God, Creator of all things, mighty and awesome, just and forgiving, you alone are good and kind. You saved Israel from all manner of plagues, making our forefathers your chosen people, and hallowing them by the touch of your Spirit. You, by the cooperation of the Holy Spirit, prepared the body and soul of the glorious Virgin Mary to be a worthy dwelling for your Son. You filled John the Baptist with the Holy Spirit, causing him to leap with joy in his mother's womb. Accept the offering of a humble spirit, and grant the heartfelt desire of your servant, N., who pleads for the safety of the child you allowed her to conceive. Guard the life that is yours; defend it from all the craft and spite of the pitiless foe. Let your gentle hand, like that of a skilled physician, aid her delivery, bringing her offspring safe and sound to the light of day. May her child live to be reborn in holy baptism, and continuing always in your service, be found worthy of attaining everlasting life; through Christ our Lord. Amen.

BLESSING OF A WOMAN

AFTER CHILDBIRTH WHERE THE CHILD WAS STILLBORN OR DIED AFTER BIRTH

Almighty, everlasting God, lover of holy purity, who chose in your wisdom and goodness to call this woman's child to your heavenly kingdom, be pleased also, O Lord, to show your mercy to this servant of yours, comforting her with your love, helping her to accept bravely your holy will. Thus comforted by the merits of your sacred passion, and aided by the intercession of blessed Mary, ever a Virgin, and of all the saints, may she be united at last with her child for all eternity in the kingdom of heaven. We ask this of you who live and reign forever and ever. Amen.

BLESSING OF AN ADULT⁺

Lord God we present N., to you. We stand in intercession for him (her) this day asking your richest blessings for his (her) life. Grant, O Lord that he (she) may know your will, follow your plan and enjoy every grace needed to execute fully and in peace and joy the responsibilities of his (her) life. We ask this in the name of Jesus our Lord. Amen.

BLESSING OF A SICK ADULT

We entreat you, Lord, to look with favor on your servant who is weak and failing, and revive the soul you have created. Chastened by suffering may he (she) know that he (she) has been saved by your healing; through Christ our Lord. Amen.

Merciful Lord, consoler of all who believe in you, we appeal to your boundless compassion that at my humble visit you will also visit this servant of yours, lying on his (her) bed of pain, as you visited the mother-in-law of Simon Peter. Graciously stand by him (her), Lord, so that he (she) may recover his (her) lost strength, and join with your Church in returning thanks to you, who are God, living and reigning forever and ever. Amen.

BLESSING OF A COUPLE ON THEIR WEDDING ANNIVERSARY +

O Lord, our God, we thank you for the sacrament of matrimony and for the faithfulness of this couple standing before us on this day of anniversary joy. Bless this marriage again, O Lord. Grant that both husband and wife may grow in the joyful appreciation of their union and that together they will be a sign of your faithful love to all who know them. We ask this in the name of Jesus our Lord. Amen.

BLESSING OF BREAD

Lord Jesus Christ, bread of angels, living bread for everlasting life, bless † this bread as you once blessed the five loaves in the wilderness; so that all who eat it reverently may thereby obtain the health they desire for body and soul. We ask this of you who live and reign forever and ever. Amen.

BLESSING OF WINE⁺

Lord Jesus Christ, Son of the living God, be pleased to bless this fruit of the vine which you have given as refreshment for your servants. Grant that all who drink it be reminded of your steadfast love and abundant goodness, seeing in this wine both the eternal blessing of the Messianic banquet to be enjoyed by all the faithful and the drink chosen by our Lord as a memorial of the blood He shed for us. May we bless you, O Lord, in its use. Amen.

CHRISTMAS TREE⁺

Lord God, grant your blessings on this Christmas tree. We have chosen it to symbolize the joy of the celebration of the birth of Jesus. We ask that the lights on the tree may be an effective sign of Jesus, the Light you sent into the world for our salvation. Amen.

BLESSING OF MEDICINE

God, who in a wonderful way created man and still more wondrously renewed him; who were pleased to aid with many healing remedies the various infirmities that beset the human condition; mercifully pour out your holy † blessing on this medicine, so that he (she) who takes it may have health in mind and body; through Christ our Lord. Amen.

BLESSING OF SEED

Lord, we earnestly beg you to bless † these seeds, to protect and preserve them with gentle breezes, to make them fertile with heavenly dew, and to bring them, in your benevolence, to the fullest harvest of our bodily and spiritual welfare; through Christ our Lord. Amen.

BLESSING OF FIELDS

God, from whom every good has its beginning and from whom it receives its increase, we beg you to hear our prayers, so that what we begin for your honor and glory may be brought to a happy ending by the gift of your eternal wisdom; through Christ our Lord. Amen.

BLESSING OF PLACES

These blessings should be prayed by all who use these places, at the initial time of use and thereafter on the occasion of a special or seasonal use.

BLESSING OF A HOUSE

God the Father Almighty, we fervently implore you for the sake of this home and its occupants and possessions, that you may bless † and sanctify † them, enriching them by your kindness in every way possible. Pour out on them, Lord, heavenly dew in good measure, as well as an abundance of earthly needs. Mercifully listen to their prayers, and grant that their desires be fulfilled. At our lowly coming be pleased to bless † and sanctify † this home, as you once were pleased to bless the home of Abraham, Isaac, and Jacob. Within these walls let your angels of light preside and stand watch over those who live here; through Christ our Lord. Amen.

BLESSING OF AN APARTMENT OR HOUSE

Lord God Almighty, bless † this apartment (or home), that it be the shelter of health, purity, and self-control; that there prevail here a spirit of humility, goodness, mildness, obedience to the commandments, and gratitude to God the Father, Son, and Holy Spirit. May this blessing remain on this place and on those who live here now and always. Amen.

PLACE OF BUSINESS+

O Lord our God we ask your blessings on this place of business. We set it aside under your Lordship and governance. Grant that what we do here may be done in righteousness and peace, that it may provide sufficient sustenance for our lives and our families and may further your kingdom. We command all evil influence to depart from this place in the name of Jesus and we ask that your holy angels, O Lord, guard and protect this area and all who work here through the intercession of Holy Mary and the Saints. Amen.

MEETING PLACE+

Lord God we have set aside this place for an assembly of your people. We ask your blessings on this place that it might serve affectively as an area to promote unity, peace and the furthering of your kingdom. We command in the name of Jesus all spirits of discord or evil of any sort to depart and we ask, O God, that you send your angels to guard and protect this place and all who participate in the events held here. We pray through the intercession of Holy Mother Mary and the Saints and in the name of Jesus our Lord. Amen.

USE WHEN TRAVELING

AUTOMOBILE

Lord God, be well disposed to our prayers, and bless this vehicle with your holy hand. Appoint your holy angels as an escort over it, who will always shield its passengers and keep them safe from accidents. And as once by your deacon, Philip, you bestowed faith and grace upon the Ethiopian seated in his carriage and reading Holy Writ, so also now show the way of salvation to your servants, in order that, strengthened by your grace and ever intent upon good works, they may attain, after all the successes and failures of this life, the certain happiness of everlasting life; through Christ our Lord. Amen.

BLESSING OF AIRLINE PASSENGERS

God, the salvation of those who trust in you, kindly appoint a good angel from on high as an escort for your servants who make an airplane voyage and who call on you for help. Let him shield the passengers throughout the flight and conduct them safely to their destination; through Christ our Lord. Amen.

AIRPLANE

God, who made all things for your glory, yet destined every lower being in this world for man's service, we beg you to bless † this airplane. Let it serve to carry far and wide the fame and glory of your name, and in expediting more speedily the affairs of mankind without loss and accident. And let it foster in the souls of all the faithful who travel in it a longing for the things above: through Christ our Lord. Amen.

SHIP OR BOAT

Lord, be well disposed to our prayers, and by your holy hand bless † this ship (boat) and its passengers, as you were pleased to let your blessing hover over Noah's ark in the Deluge. Reach out your hand to them, Lord, as you did to blessed Peter as he walked upon the sea. Send your holy angel from on high to watch over it and all on board, to ward off any threat of disaster, and to guide its course through calm waters to the desired port. Then after a time, when they have successfully transacted their business, may you in your loving providence bring them back with glad hearts to their own country and home. We ask this of you who lives and reigns forever and ever. Amen.

DAILY EXAMINATION OF CONSCIENCE

We recommend that the daily examination of conscience be made before retiring.

THANK GOD:

> for all the benefits you have received during the past day,
>
> and for at least one of the general great gifts He has bestowed upon you, as your creation, redemption, the Sacraments, special graces, etc.

ASK GOD'S GRACE:

> for light to know your sins,
>
> and for grace to make true acts of contrition and firm purposes of amendment.

MAKE THE EXAMINATION:

> Make the general examination of your thoughts, words, actions, and omissions.

MAKE AN ACT OF CONTRITION:

> Tell the Lord you are sorry and ask His forgiveness in an appropriate manner.

MAKE YOUR PURPOSE OF AMENDMENT:

> Looking back, select the point on which a fresh resolution is required.
>
> Looking forward, make resolutions respecting those things that most call for care and forethought, heartily commending yourself to the Sacred Heart of Jesus.

EXAMINATION OF CONSCIENCE

*Recommended before celebrating the
Sacrament of Penance*

PRAYER OF PREPARATION

Lord Jesus Christ, when you appeared
To the Apostles after your Resurrection,
You breathed on them and said,
"Receive the Holy Spirit.
If you forgive sins they are forgiven." *John 20:21*

Your beloved disciple, John, teaches us
That if we acknowledge our sins you,
Who are just, can be trusted to forgive
Our sins and cleanse us from every wrong.

1 John 1:9

Your disciple, James, has taught us to
Declare our sins and to pray that we
May find healing. *James 5:16*

In obedience to you and your Church
I come to this Sacrament of Penance
Seeking your mercy and forgiveness.
Enlighten my mind and heart
That I may make a good confession
And experience your healing love.
Amen.

I. I am the Lord your God, you shall not
have strange gods before me.

Do I love God above all else?

Do I put anything or anyone ahead of
Him: money, power, sex, a particular
person?

Do I blame God when I am dissatisfied?

In what manner have I performed my daily prayers, Holy Mass, other pious practices such as the Rosary, spiritual reading, Eucharistic adoration?

Have I dealt with the occult, spiritists, fortune tellers, horoscopes, or other related things such as tarot cards, ouija boards, card or palm readers?

II. You shall not take the name of the Lord your God in vain.

Have I sworn falsely?

Have I used profanity?

Have I used the name of Jesus irreverently?

III. Remember to keep holy the Lord's day.

Have I participated in the celebration of Mass every Sunday and on Holy Days of Obligation?

Have I treated Sunday like any other day?

IV. Honor your father and mother.

Do I respect my parents and all in authority?

Do I support my parents according to their need?

V. You shall not kill.

Have I injured or endangered anyone by anger, drunkenness or carelessness?

Have I used harmful or addictive drugs?

Have I used alcohol to excess?

Have I advised, procured or participated in abortion or euthanasia?

VI. You shall not commit adultery.

Has there been any fault in thought, word or act concerning all or any sexual activity outside of marriage, alone or with another?

Have I put myself in occasions of sin through what I read or view, through the company I keep, the relationships I have developed, the places I go, or the thoughts I entertain?

VII. You shall not steal.

Have I taken or withheld what belongs to another?

Have I damaged the property of others?

Have I used my resources well to support the Church, those in need, and to pay a just wage for services and goods?

Have I lived up to my commitments on my job, used my time well?

VIII. You shall not bear false witness against your neighbor.

Have I lied about anyone?

Have I damaged anyone's reputation in ways I could have avoided?

Have I judged anyone rashly?

IX. You shall not covet your neighbor's wife.

Have I respected the marriage bonds of others, even in my thoughts?

Have I engaged in impure fantasies and desires?

X. You shall not covet your neighbor's goods.

Have I been a good steward of all goods, property and profits entrusted in my care?

Have I been jealous or envious?

Have I been mean or petty toward those who have more than I?

Also: In regards to your state of life: student, single, celibate, married; your covenants and promises to the Lord:

My duties: Have I neglected them? Put them off? Done them badly?

Have I labored devotedly? Thoroughly? Impartially towards all? In a spirit of faith and love?

Have I served Christ in my job, family, friends? With constancy? With kindness?

INDULGENCES

Indulgences are a channel of the merciful love of God which frees us from the consequences of sin which remain even after the sin has been forgiven.

God desires to remove the consequences of sin by responding to the prayers and acts of mercy or charity offered to Him by His people. The Catholic Church recognizes the value of certain prayers and good works in remitting such consequences by designating specific indulgences obtainable through the prayers and good works.

Indulgences are either "plenary," removing all consequences of sin that result in God's punishment, or "partial," removing part of the consequences of sin.

We may seek indulgences either for ourselves or for others, including the deceased who may still be in purgatory. To gain an indulgence we must "love God, detest sin, place our trust in the merits of Christ, and believe firmly in the great assistance we derive from the communion of saints" (Apostolic Constitution on the Doctrine of Indulgences, January 1, 1967, No. 10).

To gain a plenary indulgence we must also participate in the sacrament of penance, receive Holy Communion, and pray for the intentions of the Holy Father, along with carrying out the prescribed prayer or work to which the indulgence is attached.

INDEX

PRAYERS

BLESSINGS